# Overheard
# in
# Love

Yep! This is the guy I've searched my whole life for!

# *Overheard*
# in
# Love

## *Judith Henry*

UNIVERSE

First published in the United States of America in 2001
by UNIVERSE PUBLISHING
A Division of Rizzoli International Publications, Inc.
300 Park Avenue South
New York, NY 10010

The text in this book does not necessarily express the sentiments of
the pictured subjects.

2001 2002 2003 2004 2005 / 10 9 8 7 6 5 4 3 2 1

Design and photography by Judith Henry

Printed in Singapore

## Introduction

Young or old, married, single, or gay, everyone seems to have something to say about love.

During my many years of eavesdropping, I have overheard plenty about relationships. Whenever someone is talking I move in to listen. People everywhere are discussing their love lives. Poets and songwriters throughout the ages have written about love and intimacy. But this book is different. These words have been spoken by ordinary people in everyday circumstances to their friends and lovers.

What I hear is sometimes humorous, sometimes sad, hopeful, or jaded, but always poignant.

People are longing to love and be loved.

J. H.

It was like the most romantic moment in my life.

Tick-tock, I'm thirty-five years old already, ya know.

Tell me you love me, tell me you love me just one more time.

I've had flirtations, but I've always been faithful to John.

He worships me!

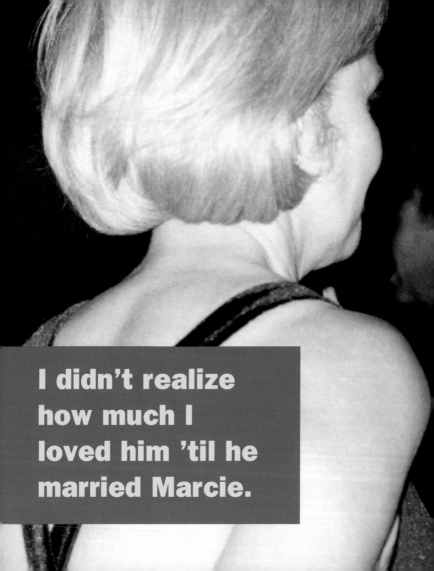

**Sam, if you were really romantic you would have proposed by e-mail.**

At last, we stopped hurting each other.

The answer is,
to lie to her.

There are a lot of cute faces, cute penises, cute butts, but sooner or later you have to choose.

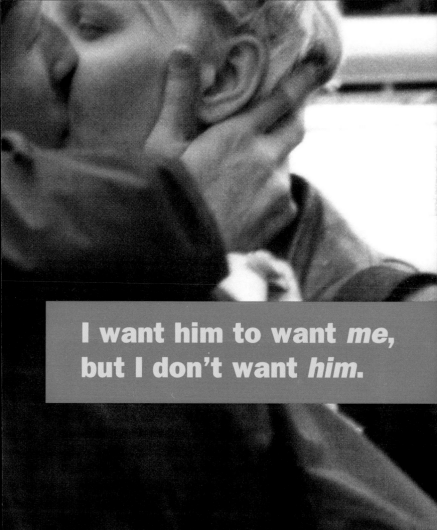

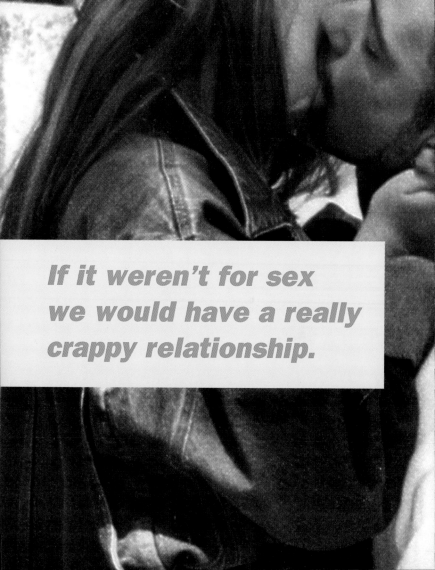

He's all she can ever talk about.

Sara just lives
to get married.

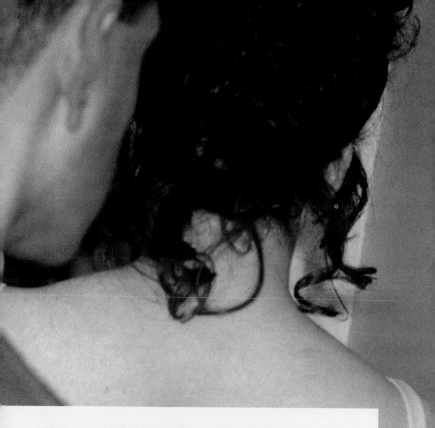

**Even though we're completely incompatible, we're happy together.**

She can always
make me smile.

*Despite all that—
we've had twenty
glorious years!*

Sure, he's sweet and good-looking, but he's shorter than me.

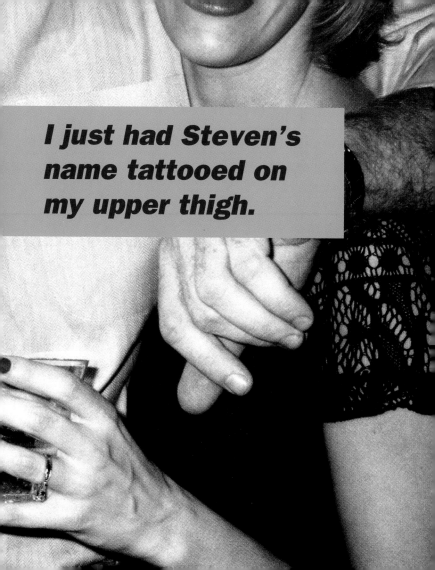

I'd call that platonic cuddling.

I love romantic movies—
they give me hope.

I plan to have a really spectacular wedding— if Peter ever agrees to marry me!

It's more fun flirting than dating.

*Let's talk about us.*

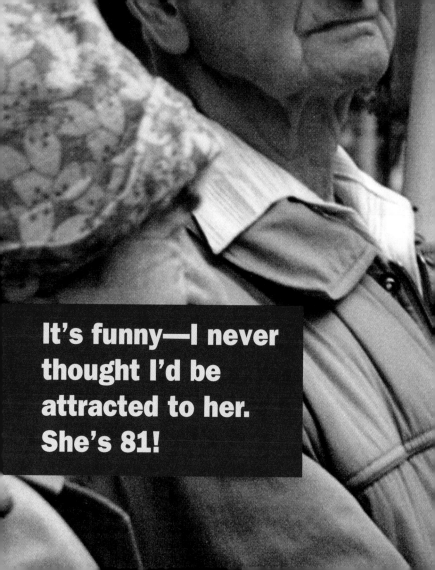

I thought you said
you wanted to
spend the rest of
your life with me.

Come on Sue, give me a second chance.

I'm in love with someone who is totally wrong for me.

OK Mimi, so I don't *always* treat you so well.

Why is he with Bev
instead of Diana?

Ya gotta make me feel secure—ya gotta tell me you love me!

*After he proposed, I took two weeks to think about it.*

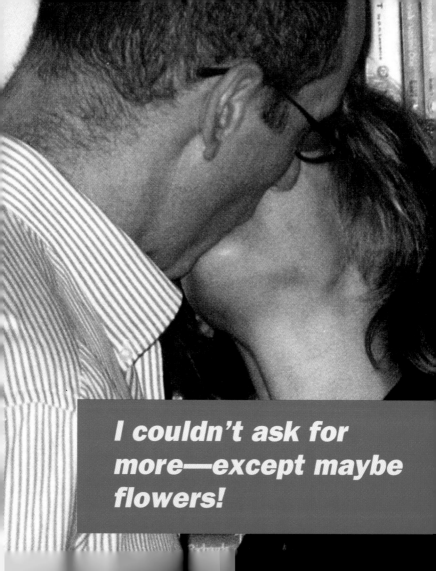

**And everyone thought we were the perfect couple.**

I'm the only idiot that would date you.

*Wait 'til I tell you how Adam proposed.*

So that's why you stay with me!

I've been carrying on an affair of fantasy for the past year.

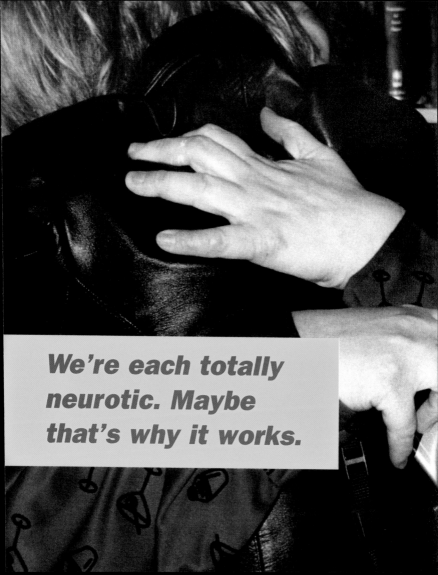

I don't want to ruin our relationship with a relationship.

I wonder if we'll be this happy ten years from now.

The closest we came
to a break was when I
slept with her girlfriend
Maggie.

Are you going to go on and on or do you want me to make it up to you?

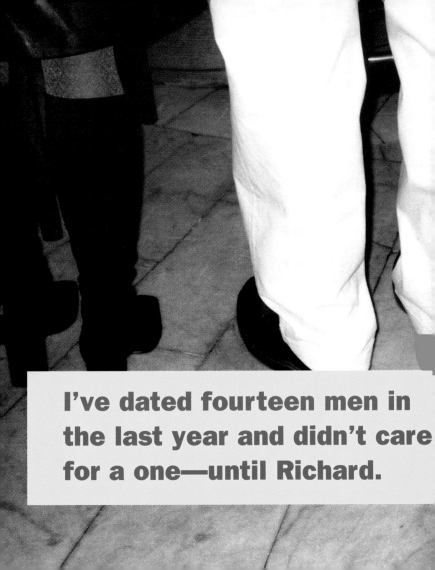

I've dated fourteen men in the last year and didn't care for a one—until Richard.

We got the invitations out immediately so he couldn't change his mind.

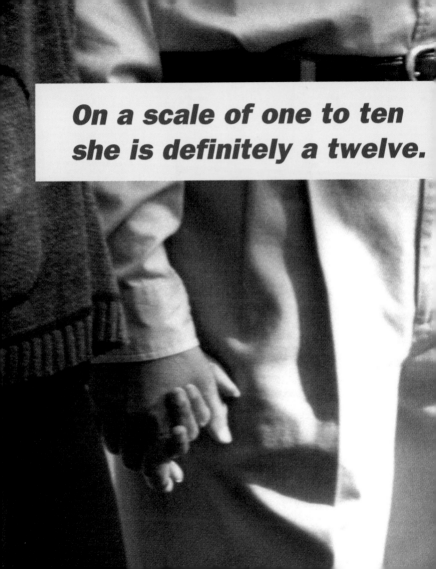

Baby, I'm so happy you said yes tonight!

**It's finally time for my dreams to come true.**

## About the Author

Judith Henry's art has been exhibited internationally in New York, Barcelona, Buenos Aires, and London among other places. She also designed works for The Museum of Modern Art, New York. In 1997 her book *Anonymous True Stories* was published. In 2000-01 Universe published her books, *Overheard at the Museum*, *Overheard at the Bookstore* and *Overheard While Shopping.* She lives in New York City.